Gospel Journey

Full Year Version

Gospel Journey, Full Year Version
Verna McCrillis and Beth Warlick
Copyright © 2017 Establishing God's Peace

Unless otherwise indicated, Scripture quotations are from the ESV Bible. (The Holy Bible, English Standard Version.)

Cover photo by Erin Joy Turkington

Prepared for publication by Katherine McCrillis

Gospel Journey, an inductive devotional guide, is designed to encourage growth in:
1) knowing who God is
2) knowing who I am apart from God
3) knowing who I am in Christ
4) trusting Him moment by moment through the Spirit

God can use this unique tool to revitalize and strengthen your Christian walk. It was designed to encourage you to get to know God as He reveals Himself through His Word and to view life through the lens of the gospel.

As you are faithful (by His grace) to keep rediscovering, reinforcing and practicing the things God has taught you, He can use this journal to remind you of His truths as He grows your faith and establishes His peace in your life.

Our hope is that as a result of spending time with God in His Word and in prayer, the Holy Spirit will convince you of who the Triune God is. And, as you come to know and trust God intimately, you will become more aware of your need for Him and for Jesus, His Son. He promises to give you the grace to grow in appreciation for the great salvation Christ has provided.

You can use "The Tabernacle" on the next page to help remember the gospel each day. The chart in the back section, "What Do I Believe?" is a tool that can help you grow in moving toward God through your awareness of the gospel.

Remembering the Gospel

In Hebrews 8-10 we see that the Old Testament Tabernacle (summarized in Exodus 40) was given as a shadow or a foreshadowing of what was to come—Jesus.

The picture of the Old Testament tabernacle fulfilled in Christ is a tool that can help us remember the gospel and enable us to "fix our eyes on Jesus" (Hebrews 12:2).

God used the Old Testament Tabernacle to explain the work of Christ that gives us free access to God. Many verses in the New Testament describing Jesus correspond to different parts of the tabernacle. We can use these verses to praise God for providing the one and only way to come to Him, praising Jesus for being the Lamb of God that took away our sin, our cleansing, our bread of life, etc. all the way to boldly coming to the throne of grace to receive His mercy and grace in this time of need.

This is a word picture to help us remember the gospel. As we remember with awe that God provided a way to come into His very presence through Jesus, gratitude for our great salvation may result.

A section with a cross is provided in the Profess column where we can also note all the different aspects of the gospel as we are reading Scripture.

1. **The only door** John 10:7-9
   Jesus said, "I am the door."

2. **Altar of sacrifice** John 1:29
   "Behold the Lamb of God Who takes away the sin of the world."

3. **Bronze basin, for washing** 1 John 1:7
   "the blood of Jesus His Son, cleanses us from all sins."

4. **The bread of the Presence** John 6:35
   "I am the bread of life; he who comes to Me shall not hunger."

5. **Lampstand** John 8:12
   "I am the light of the world."

6. **Incense** Hebrews 7:25
   "He always lives to intercede for them (those who come to God through Him)." Rev. 5:8 Incense is a symbol of prayer.

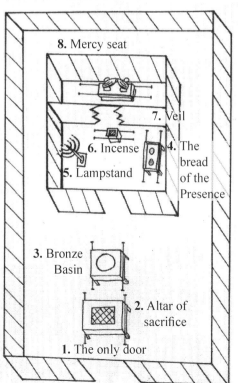

7. **Veil** Hebrews 10:19-20
   "We have confidence to enter the holy place by the blood of Jesus... through the veil, that is, His flesh."

8. **Mercy seat** Hebrews 4:16
   "Let us therefore draw near with confidence to the throne of grace, that we may receive mercy and may find grace to help in time of need."

"How great is the love the Father has lavished on us
that we should be called children of God! And this is what we are!"
1 John 3:1

Peace through the Word and Prayer

Example:

This journal has places to record the things God is impressing on you as you read Scripture. (A daily Scripture reading recommendation is provided at the end of this section if you don't already have one.) It may help you intentionally take time to get to know the Triune God by following these steps:

1. As you begin to read a passage, invite God to teach you about His character from the passage.

2. Mark every mention of "God" as you read.

   (Example)
   Mark each mention of God with a color or symbol as you read.

   God   Jesus   Holy Spirit

3. Note ONE thing that stood out about God's character from the passage and write it in the **Praise** section. Use this truth to praise God. As the week progresses, you can review the other things you have already written and your praise will grow.

4. If the Holy Spirit impresses you with specific truths that you need to acknowledge about yourself, note them in the **Profess** section along with the passage reference. This will provide a place to ask God to enable you to believe that truth.

5. You can use the **Requests** and **Thanks** sections to note the other things you want to pray about and follow up with thanksgiving when you see His answers. (The scriptural understanding of thanks is to acknowledge that you are "well-graced.")

Week of March 11–17 Daily Scripture Reading	11 Sunday ✓ Psalm 30–31	12 Monday ✓ Devt. 3–4	13 Tuesday Devt. 5–6
14 Wednesday Devt. 5–6	15 Thursday Devt. 5–6	16 Friday Devt. 5–6	17 Saturday Devt. 5–6

Praise How does scripture describe God?

Ps. 31:5 — You are a God of truth and faithfulness.
You are the redeemer.

Devt. 3:22 — The Lord my God is the One fighting for me.

Devt. 4:24 — You are a jealous God, a consuming fire.

Devt. 5:10 — God, You show loving-kindness to 1000s and
to those who love You and keep Your commandments.

Devt. 7:9 — Know that the LORD is God, faithful
(You keep Your covenants.)

Devt. 7:21 — You are a great and awesome God!

Profess
What specific truth is God encouraging me to acknowledge?

Ps. 30:1 — "You have lifted me up and have not let my enemies rejoice over me!" FEAR NOT!

God is fighting for me. (Deut 3:22)

Deut. 4:35 — God shows Himself that I may know Him and KNOW that He is God.

This box can be used to note either the gospel or things that I may want to add to the Grace Exchange section. Examples of both are below.

Pondering the Gospel or Grace Exchange

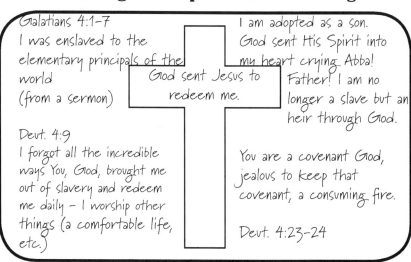

Galatians 4:1-7
I was enslaved to the elementary principals of the world
(from a sermon)

God sent Jesus to redeem me.

I am adopted as a son. God sent His Spirit into my heart crying Abba! Father! I am no longer a slave but an heir through God.

Deut. 4:9
I forgot all the incredible ways You, God, brought me out of slavery and redeem me daily — I worship other things (a comfortable life, etc.)

You are a covenant God, jealous to keep that covenant, a consuming fire.

Deut. 4:23-24

Requests
Make my requests known to God with praise and thanksgiving.

Ps. 31:32— As I deal with this financial crunch, cause me to be strong, take courage and trust in You as Provider.
Cause me to believe that You provide safety for my husband while he travels.

Thanks
Give thanks to God, acknowledging His abundant grace in the midst of the situation, even when I don't understand.

Thank You for providing all the grace I need in this financial crunch — I see how You are drawing me to Yourself through it.
(When God answers the prayer about giving me peace for my husband's safety while traveling, I can come back to this section and note it and thank God for His grace, even if the outcome is different than I was expecting.)

Week of _____ Daily Scripture Reading	Sunday	Monday	Tuesday
Wednesday	Thursday	Friday	Saturday

Praise How does scripture describe God?

_____
_____
_____
_____
_____
_____
_____
_____
_____
_____
_____
_____
_____
_____
_____
_____
_____
_____
_____
_____
_____
_____
_____
_____
_____

Profess What specific truth is God encouraging me to acknowledge?

Pondering the Gospel or Grace Exchange

Requests

Make my requests known to God with praise and thanksgiving.

_____
_____
_____
_____
_____
_____
_____
_____
_____
_____
_____
_____
_____
_____
_____
_____
_____
_____
_____
_____
_____
_____
_____
_____
_____
_____
_____
_____

Thanks

Give thanks to God, acknowledging His abundant grace in the midst of the situation, even when I don't understand.

_____
_____
_____
_____
_____
_____
_____
_____
_____
_____
_____
_____
_____
_____
_____
_____
_____
_____
_____
_____
_____
_____
_____
_____
_____
_____
_____
_____

Week of _____ Daily Scripture Reading	Sunday	Monday	Tuesday
Wednesday	Thursday	Friday	Saturday

Praise How does scripture describe God?

_____
_____
_____
_____
_____
_____
_____
_____
_____
_____
_____
_____
_____
_____
_____
_____
_____
_____
_____
_____
_____
_____
_____

Profess
What specific truth is God encouraging me to acknowledge?

_____
_____
_____
_____
_____
_____
_____
_____
_____
_____
_____
_____
_____
_____
_____
_____

Pondering the Gospel or Grace Exchange

Requests
Make my requests known to God with praise and thanksgiving.

Thanks
Give thanks to God, acknowledging His abundant grace in the midst of the situation, even when I don't understand.

Week of _____ Daily Scripture Reading	Sunday	Monday	Tuesday
Wednesday	Thursday	Friday	Saturday

Praise How does scripture describe God?

Profess What specific truth is God encouraging me to acknowledge?

_____
_____
_____
_____
_____
_____
_____
_____
_____
_____
_____
_____
_____
_____
_____
_____

Pondering the Gospel or Grace Exchange

Requests

Make my requests known to God with praise and thanksgiving.

Thanks

Give thanks to God, acknowledging His abundant grace in the midst of the situation, even when I don't understand.

Week of _____ Daily Scripture Reading	Sunday	Monday	Tuesday
Wednesday	Thursday	Friday	Saturday

Praise How does scripture describe God?

Profess
What specific truth is God encouraging me to acknowledge?

_____
_____
_____
_____
_____
_____
_____
_____
_____
_____
_____
_____
_____
_____
_____
_____

Pondering the Gospel or Grace Exchange

Requests
Make my requests known to God with praise and thanksgiving.

Thanks
Give thanks to God, acknowledging His abundant grace in the midst of the situation, even when I don't understand.

Week of _____ Daily Scripture Reading	Sunday	Monday	Tuesday
Wednesday	Thursday	Friday	Saturday

Praise How does scripture describe God?

_____
_____
_____
_____
_____
_____
_____
_____
_____
_____
_____
_____
_____
_____
_____
_____
_____
_____
_____
_____
_____
_____

Profess What specific truth is God encouraging me to acknowledge?

_____
_____
_____
_____
_____
_____
_____
_____
_____
_____
_____
_____
_____
_____
_____
_____

Pondering the Gospel or Grace Exchange

Requests

Make my requests known to God with praise and thanksgiving.

_____
_____
_____
_____
_____
_____
_____
_____
_____
_____
_____
_____
_____
_____
_____
_____
_____
_____
_____
_____
_____
_____
_____
_____
_____
_____
_____

Thanks

Give thanks to God, acknowledging His abundant grace in the midst of the situation, even when I don't understand.

_____
_____
_____
_____
_____
_____
_____
_____
_____
_____
_____
_____
_____
_____
_____
_____
_____
_____
_____
_____
_____
_____
_____
_____
_____
_____
_____

Week of _____ Daily Scripture Reading	Sunday	Monday	Tuesday
Wednesday	Thursday	Friday	Saturday

Praise How does scripture describe God?

Profess What specific truth is God encouraging me to acknowledge?

_____
_____
_____
_____
_____
_____
_____
_____
_____
_____
_____
_____
_____
_____
_____

Pondering the Gospel or Grace Exchange

Requests

Make my requests known to God with praise and thanksgiving.

Thanks

Give thanks to God, acknowledging His abundant grace in the midst of the situation, even when I don't understand.

Week of _____ Daily Scripture Reading	Sunday	Monday	Tuesday
Wednesday	Thursday	Friday	Saturday

Praise How does scripture describe God?

Profess What specific truth is God encouraging me to acknowledge?

_____
_____
_____
_____
_____
_____
_____
_____
_____
_____
_____
_____
_____
_____
_____
_____

Pondering the Gospel or Grace Exchange

Requests
Make my requests known to God with praise and thanksgiving.

_____
_____
_____
_____
_____
_____
_____
_____
_____
_____
_____
_____
_____
_____
_____
_____
_____
_____
_____
_____
_____
_____
_____
_____
_____
_____
_____
_____

Thanks
Give thanks to God, acknowledging His abundant grace in the midst of the situation, even when I don't understand.

_____
_____
_____
_____
_____
_____
_____
_____
_____
_____
_____
_____
_____
_____
_____
_____
_____
_____
_____
_____
_____
_____
_____
_____
_____
_____
_____
_____

Week of _____ Daily Scripture Reading	Sunday	Monday	Tuesday
Wednesday	Thursday	Friday	Saturday

Praise How does scripture describe God?

_____
_____
_____
_____
_____
_____
_____
_____
_____
_____
_____
_____
_____
_____
_____
_____
_____
_____
_____
_____
_____
_____

Profess
What specific truth is God encouraging me to acknowledge?

_____
_____
_____
_____
_____
_____
_____
_____
_____
_____
_____
_____
_____
_____
_____
_____

Pondering the Gospel or Grace Exchange

Requests
Make my requests known to God with praise and thanksgiving.

Thanks
Give thanks to God, acknowledging His abundant grace in the midst of the situation, even when I don't understand.

Week of _____ Daily Scripture Reading	Sunday	Monday	Tuesday
Wednesday	Thursday	Friday	Saturday

Praise How does scripture describe God?

Profess
What specific truth is God encouraging me to acknowledge?

_____
_____
_____
_____
_____
_____
_____
_____
_____
_____
_____
_____
_____
_____
_____
_____

Pondering the Gospel or Grace Exchange

Requests
Make my requests known to God with praise and thanksgiving.

Thanks
Give thanks to God, acknowledging His abundant grace in the midst of the situation, even when I don't understand.

Week of _____ Daily Scripture Reading	Sunday	Monday	Tuesday
Wednesday	Thursday	Friday	Saturday

Praise How does scripture describe God?

Profess What specific truth is God encouraging me to acknowledge?

_____
_____
_____
_____
_____
_____
_____
_____
_____
_____
_____
_____
_____
_____
_____
_____

Pondering the Gospel or Grace Exchange

Requests

Make my requests known to God with praise and thanksgiving.

Thanks

Give thanks to God, acknowledging His abundant grace in the midst of the situation, even when I don't understand.

Week of _____ Daily Scripture Reading	Sunday	Monday	Tuesday
Wednesday	Thursday	Friday	Saturday

Praise How does scripture describe God?

Profess
What specific truth is God encouraging me to acknowledge?

_____
_____
_____
_____
_____
_____
_____
_____
_____
_____
_____
_____
_____
_____
_____

Pondering the Gospel or Grace Exchange

Requests

Make my requests known to God with praise and thanksgiving.

_____
_____
_____
_____
_____
_____
_____
_____
_____
_____
_____
_____
_____
_____
_____
_____
_____
_____
_____
_____
_____
_____
_____
_____
_____
_____
_____
_____
_____
_____

Thanks

Give thanks to God, acknowledging His abundant grace in the midst of the situation, even when I don't understand.

_____
_____
_____
_____
_____
_____
_____
_____
_____
_____
_____
_____
_____
_____
_____
_____
_____
_____
_____
_____
_____
_____
_____
_____
_____
_____
_____
_____
_____
_____

Week of _____ Daily Scripture Reading	Sunday	Monday	Tuesday
Wednesday	Thursday	Friday	Saturday

Praise How does scripture describe God?

_____
_____
_____
_____
_____
_____
_____
_____
_____
_____
_____
_____
_____
_____
_____
_____
_____
_____
_____
_____
_____
_____
_____
_____
_____

Profess
What specific truth is God encouraging me to acknowledge?

_____
_____
_____
_____
_____
_____
_____
_____
_____
_____
_____
_____
_____
_____
_____
_____

Pondering the Gospel or Grace Exchange

Requests
Make my requests known to God with praise and thanksgiving.

_____
_____
_____
_____
_____
_____
_____
_____
_____
_____
_____
_____
_____
_____
_____
_____
_____
_____
_____
_____
_____
_____
_____
_____
_____
_____

Thanks
Give thanks to God, acknowledging His abundant grace in the midst of the situation, even when I don't understand.

_____
_____
_____
_____
_____
_____
_____
_____
_____
_____
_____
_____
_____
_____
_____
_____
_____
_____
_____
_____
_____
_____
_____
_____
_____
_____

Week of _____ Daily Scripture Reading	Sunday	Monday	Tuesday
Wednesday	Thursday	Friday	Saturday

Praise How does scripture describe God?

_____
_____
_____
_____
_____
_____
_____
_____
_____
_____
_____
_____
_____
_____
_____
_____
_____
_____
_____
_____
_____
_____
_____

Profess What specific truth is God encouraging me to acknowledge?

_____
_____
_____
_____
_____
_____
_____
_____
_____
_____
_____
_____
_____
_____
_____

Pondering the Gospel or Grace Exchange

Requests

Make my requests known to God with praise and thanksgiving.

_____
_____
_____
_____
_____
_____
_____
_____
_____
_____
_____
_____
_____
_____
_____
_____
_____
_____
_____
_____
_____
_____
_____
_____
_____
_____
_____
_____

Thanks

Give thanks to God, acknowledging His abundant grace in the midst of the situation, even when I don't understand.

_____
_____
_____
_____
_____
_____
_____
_____
_____
_____
_____
_____
_____
_____
_____
_____
_____
_____
_____
_____
_____
_____
_____
_____
_____
_____
_____
_____

Week of Daily Scripture Reading	Sunday	Monday	Tuesday
Wednesday	Thursday	Friday	Saturday

Praise How does scripture describe God?

Profess
What specific truth is God encouraging me to acknowledge?

_____
_____
_____
_____
_____
_____
_____
_____
_____
_____
_____
_____
_____
_____
_____

Pondering the Gospel or Grace Exchange

Requests
Make my requests known to God with praise and thanksgiving.

_____
_____
_____
_____
_____
_____
_____
_____
_____
_____
_____
_____
_____
_____
_____
_____
_____
_____
_____
_____
_____
_____
_____
_____
_____
_____
_____
_____

Thanks
Give thanks to God, acknowledging His abundant grace in the midst of the situation, even when I don't understand.

_____
_____
_____
_____
_____
_____
_____
_____
_____
_____
_____
_____
_____
_____
_____
_____
_____
_____
_____
_____
_____
_____
_____
_____
_____
_____
_____
_____

Week of _____ Daily Scripture Reading	Sunday	Monday	Tuesday
Wednesday	Thursday	Friday	Saturday

Praise How does scripture describe God?

Profess
What specific truth is God encouraging me to acknowledge?

_____
_____
_____
_____
_____
_____
_____
_____
_____
_____
_____
_____
_____
_____
_____

Pondering the Gospel or Grace Exchange

Requests

Make my requests known to God with praise and thanksgiving.

_____
_____
_____
_____
_____
_____
_____
_____
_____
_____
_____
_____
_____
_____
_____
_____
_____
_____
_____
_____
_____
_____
_____
_____
_____
_____
_____
_____

Thanks

Give thanks to God, acknowledging His abundant grace in the midst of the situation, even when I don't understand.

_____
_____
_____
_____
_____
_____
_____
_____
_____
_____
_____
_____
_____
_____
_____
_____
_____
_____
_____
_____
_____
_____
_____
_____
_____
_____
_____
_____

Week of _____ Daily Scripture Reading	Sunday	Monday	Tuesday
Wednesday	Thursday	Friday	Saturday

Praise How does scripture describe God?

Profess
What specific truth is God encouraging me to acknowledge?

_____
_____
_____
_____
_____
_____
_____
_____
_____
_____
_____
_____
_____
_____
_____
_____
_____

Pondering the Gospel or Grace Exchange

Requests
Make my requests known to God with praise and thanksgiving.

_____
_____
_____
_____
_____
_____
_____
_____
_____
_____
_____
_____
_____
_____
_____
_____
_____
_____
_____
_____
_____
_____
_____
_____
_____
_____
_____

Thanks
Give thanks to God, acknowledging His abundant grace in the midst of the situation, even when I don't understand.

_____
_____
_____
_____
_____
_____
_____
_____
_____
_____
_____
_____
_____
_____
_____
_____
_____
_____
_____
_____
_____
_____
_____
_____
_____
_____
_____

Week of _____ Daily Scripture Reading	Sunday	Monday	Tuesday
Wednesday	Thursday	Friday	Saturday

Praise How does scripture describe God?

_____
_____
_____
_____
_____
_____
_____
_____
_____
_____
_____
_____
_____
_____
_____
_____
_____
_____
_____
_____
_____
_____
_____

Profess What specific truth is God encouraging me to acknowledge?

_____
_____
_____
_____
_____
_____
_____
_____
_____
_____
_____
_____
_____
_____
_____

Pondering the Gospel or Grace Exchange

Requests
Make my requests known to God with praise and thanksgiving.

Thanks
Give thanks to God, acknowledging His abundant grace in the midst of the situation, even when I don't understand.

Week of _____ Daily Scripture Reading	Sunday	Monday	Tuesday
Wednesday	Thursday	Friday	Saturday

Praise How does scripture describe God?

_____
_____
_____
_____
_____
_____
_____
_____
_____
_____
_____
_____
_____
_____
_____
_____
_____
_____
_____
_____
_____
_____
_____
_____

Profess What specific truth is God encouraging me to acknowledge?

_____
_____
_____
_____
_____
_____
_____
_____
_____
_____
_____
_____
_____
_____
_____
_____

Pondering the Gospel or Grace Exchange

Requests
Make my requests known to God with praise and thanksgiving.

Thanks
Give thanks to God, acknowledging His abundant grace in the midst of the situation, even when I don't understand.

Week of _____ Daily Scripture Reading	Sunday	Monday	Tuesday
Wednesday	Thursday	Friday	Saturday

Praise How does scripture describe God?

Profess
What specific truth is God encouraging me to acknowledge?

_____
_____
_____
_____
_____
_____
_____
_____
_____
_____
_____
_____
_____
_____
_____
_____
_____

Pondering the Gospel or Grace Exchange

Requests
Make my requests known to God with praise and thanksgiving.

_____
_____
_____
_____
_____
_____
_____
_____
_____
_____
_____
_____
_____
_____
_____
_____
_____
_____
_____
_____
_____
_____
_____
_____
_____
_____
_____
_____
_____

Thanks
Give thanks to God, acknowledging His abundant grace in the midst of the situation, even when I don't understand.

_____
_____
_____
_____
_____
_____
_____
_____
_____
_____
_____
_____
_____
_____
_____
_____
_____
_____
_____
_____
_____
_____
_____
_____
_____
_____
_____
_____

Week of	Sunday	Monday	Tuesday
Daily Scripture Reading			
Wednesday	Thursday	Friday	Saturday

Praise How does scripture describe God?

_____
_____
_____
_____
_____
_____
_____
_____
_____
_____
_____
_____
_____
_____
_____
_____
_____
_____
_____
_____

Profess
What specific truth is God encouraging me to acknowledge?

_____
_____
_____
_____
_____
_____
_____
_____
_____
_____
_____
_____
_____
_____
_____

Pondering the Gospel or Grace Exchange

Requests
Make my requests known to God with praise and thanksgiving.

Thanks
Give thanks to God, acknowledging His abundant grace in the midst of the situation, even when I don't understand.

Week of _____ Daily Scripture Reading	Sunday	Monday	Tuesday
Wednesday	Thursday	Friday	Saturday

Praise How does scripture describe God?

_____
_____
_____
_____
_____
_____
_____
_____
_____
_____
_____
_____
_____
_____
_____
_____
_____
_____
_____
_____
_____
_____
_____
_____

Profess
What specific truth is God encouraging me to acknowledge?

_____
_____
_____
_____
_____
_____
_____
_____
_____
_____
_____
_____
_____
_____
_____
_____

Pondering the Gospel or Grace Exchange

Requests

Make my requests known to God with praise and thanksgiving.

_____
_____
_____
_____
_____
_____
_____
_____
_____
_____
_____
_____
_____
_____
_____
_____
_____
_____
_____
_____
_____
_____
_____
_____
_____
_____

Thanks

Give thanks to God, acknowledging His abundant grace in the midst of the situation, even when I don't understand.

_____
_____
_____
_____
_____
_____
_____
_____
_____
_____
_____
_____
_____
_____
_____
_____
_____
_____
_____
_____
_____
_____
_____
_____
_____
_____

Week of _____ Daily Scripture Reading	Sunday	Monday	Tuesday
Wednesday	Thursday	Friday	Saturday

Praise How does scripture describe God?

_____
_____
_____
_____
_____
_____
_____
_____
_____
_____
_____
_____
_____
_____
_____
_____
_____
_____
_____
_____
_____

Profess — What specific truth is God encouraging me to acknowledge?

_____
_____
_____
_____
_____
_____
_____
_____
_____
_____
_____
_____
_____
_____
_____

Pondering the Gospel or Grace Exchange

Requests
Make my requests known to God with praise and thanksgiving.

Thanks
Give thanks to God, acknowledging His abundant grace in the midst of the situation, even when I don't understand.

Week of _____ Daily Scripture Reading	Sunday	Monday	Tuesday
Wednesday	Thursday	Friday	Saturday

Praise How does scripture describe God?

_____
_____
_____
_____
_____
_____
_____
_____
_____
_____
_____
_____
_____
_____
_____
_____
_____
_____
_____
_____
_____
_____

Profess What specific truth is God encouraging me to acknowledge?

_____
_____
_____
_____
_____
_____
_____
_____
_____
_____
_____
_____
_____
_____
_____
_____

Pondering the Gospel or Grace Exchange

Requests

Make my requests known to God with praise and thanksgiving.

_____

Thanks

Give thanks to God, acknowledging His abundant grace in the midst of the situation, even when I don't understand.

_____

Week of	Sunday	Monday	Tuesday
Daily Scripture Reading			
Wednesday	Thursday	Friday	Saturday

Praise How does scripture describe God?

Profess What specific truth is God encouraging me to acknowledge?

_____
_____
_____
_____
_____
_____
_____
_____
_____
_____
_____
_____
_____
_____
_____
_____

Pondering the Gospel or Grace Exchange

Requests

Make my requests known to God with praise and thanksgiving.

_____
_____
_____
_____
_____
_____
_____
_____
_____
_____
_____
_____
_____
_____
_____
_____
_____
_____
_____
_____
_____
_____
_____
_____
_____
_____

Thanks

Give thanks to God, acknowledging His abundant grace in the midst of the situation, even when I don't understand.

_____
_____
_____
_____
_____
_____
_____
_____
_____
_____
_____
_____
_____
_____
_____
_____
_____
_____
_____
_____
_____
_____
_____
_____
_____
_____

Week of _____ Daily Scripture Reading	Sunday	Monday	Tuesday
Wednesday	Thursday	Friday	Saturday

Praise How does scripture describe God?

Profess
What specific truth is God encouraging me to acknowledge?

_____
_____
_____
_____
_____
_____
_____
_____
_____
_____
_____
_____
_____
_____
_____

Pondering the Gospel or Grace Exchange

Requests

Make my requests known to God with praise and thanksgiving.

Thanks

Give thanks to God, acknowledging His abundant grace in the midst of the situation, even when I don't understand.

Week of _____ Daily Scripture Reading	Sunday	Monday	Tuesday
Wednesday	Thursday	Friday	Saturday

Praise How does scripture describe God?

_____
_____
_____
_____
_____
_____
_____
_____
_____
_____
_____
_____
_____
_____
_____
_____
_____
_____
_____
_____
_____
_____
_____

Profess
What specific truth is God encouraging me to acknowledge?

_____
_____
_____
_____
_____
_____
_____
_____
_____
_____
_____
_____
_____
_____
_____

Pondering the Gospel or Grace Exchange

Requests

Make my requests known to God with praise and thanksgiving.

Thanks

Give thanks to God, acknowledging His abundant grace in the midst of the situation, even when I don't understand.

Week of _____ Daily Scripture Reading	Sunday	Monday	Tuesday
Wednesday	Thursday	Friday	Saturday

Praise How does scripture describe God?

_____
_____
_____
_____
_____
_____
_____
_____
_____
_____
_____
_____
_____
_____
_____
_____
_____
_____
_____
_____
_____
_____

Profess
What specific truth is God encouraging me to acknowledge?

_____
_____
_____
_____
_____
_____
_____
_____
_____
_____
_____
_____
_____
_____

Pondering the Gospel or Grace Exchange

Requests
Make my requests known to God with praise and thanksgiving.

Thanks
Give thanks to God, acknowledging His abundant grace in the midst of the situation, even when I don't understand.

Week of _____ Daily Scripture Reading	Sunday	Monday	Tuesday
Wednesday	Thursday	Friday	Saturday

Praise How does scripture describe God?

_____
_____
_____
_____
_____
_____
_____
_____
_____
_____
_____
_____
_____
_____
_____
_____
_____
_____
_____
_____
_____
_____
_____

Profess — What specific truth is God encouraging me to acknowledge?

_____
_____
_____
_____
_____
_____
_____
_____
_____
_____
_____
_____
_____
_____
_____
_____

Pondering the Gospel or Grace Exchange

Requests
Make my requests known to God with praise and thanksgiving.

_____
_____
_____
_____
_____
_____
_____
_____
_____
_____
_____
_____
_____
_____
_____
_____
_____
_____
_____
_____
_____
_____
_____
_____
_____
_____

Thanks
Give thanks to God, acknowledging His abundant grace in the midst of the situation, even when I don't understand.

_____
_____
_____
_____
_____
_____
_____
_____
_____
_____
_____
_____
_____
_____
_____
_____
_____
_____
_____
_____
_____
_____
_____
_____
_____
_____

Week of	Sunday	Monday	Tuesday
Daily Scripture Reading			
Wednesday	Thursday	Friday	Saturday

Praise How does scripture describe God?

_____
_____
_____
_____
_____
_____
_____
_____
_____
_____
_____
_____
_____
_____
_____
_____
_____
_____
_____
_____
_____
_____

Profess
What specific truth is God encouraging me to acknowledge?

_____
_____
_____
_____
_____
_____
_____
_____
_____
_____
_____
_____
_____
_____
_____
_____
_____

Pondering the Gospel or Grace Exchange

Requests

Make my requests known to God with praise and thanksgiving.

Thanks

Give thanks to God, acknowledging His abundant grace in the midst of the situation, even when I don't understand.

Week of _____ Daily Scripture Reading	Sunday	Monday	Tuesday
Wednesday	Thursday	Friday	Saturday

Praise How does scripture describe God?

_____
_____
_____
_____
_____
_____
_____
_____
_____
_____
_____
_____
_____
_____
_____
_____
_____
_____
_____
_____
_____
_____

Profess What specific truth is God encouraging me to acknowledge?

_____
_____
_____
_____
_____
_____
_____
_____
_____
_____
_____
_____
_____
_____
_____
_____

Pondering the Gospel or Grace Exchange

Requests

Make my requests known to God with praise and thanksgiving.

Thanks

Give thanks to God, acknowledging His abundant grace in the midst of the situation, even when I don't understand.

Week of _____ Daily Scripture Reading	Sunday	Monday	Tuesday
Wednesday	Thursday	Friday	Saturday

Praise How does scripture describe God?

_____
_____
_____
_____
_____
_____
_____
_____
_____
_____
_____
_____
_____
_____
_____
_____
_____
_____
_____
_____

Profess
What specific truth is God encouraging me to acknowledge?

_____
_____
_____
_____
_____
_____
_____
_____
_____
_____
_____
_____
_____
_____
_____
_____

Pondering the Gospel or Grace Exchange

Requests

Make my requests known to God with praise and thanksgiving.

_____
_____
_____
_____
_____
_____
_____
_____
_____
_____
_____
_____
_____
_____
_____
_____
_____
_____
_____
_____
_____
_____
_____
_____
_____
_____

Thanks

Give thanks to God, acknowledging His abundant grace in the midst of the situation, even when I don't understand.

_____
_____
_____
_____
_____
_____
_____
_____
_____
_____
_____
_____
_____
_____
_____
_____
_____
_____
_____
_____
_____
_____
_____
_____
_____
_____

Week of _____ Daily Scripture Reading	Sunday	Monday	Tuesday
Wednesday	Thursday	Friday	Saturday

Praise How does scripture describe God?

_____
_____
_____
_____
_____
_____
_____
_____
_____
_____
_____
_____
_____
_____
_____
_____
_____
_____
_____
_____
_____
_____

Profess
What specific truth is God encouraging me to acknowledge?

_____
_____
_____
_____
_____
_____
_____
_____
_____
_____
_____
_____
_____
_____
_____
_____

Pondering the Gospel or Grace Exchange

Requests

Make my requests known to God with praise and thanksgiving.

_____
_____
_____
_____
_____
_____
_____
_____
_____
_____
_____
_____
_____
_____
_____
_____
_____
_____
_____
_____
_____
_____

Thanks

Give thanks to God, acknowledging His abundant grace in the midst of the situation, even when I don't understand.

_____
_____
_____
_____
_____
_____
_____
_____
_____
_____
_____
_____
_____
_____
_____
_____
_____
_____
_____
_____
_____
_____

Week of _____ Daily Scripture Reading	Sunday	Monday	Tuesday
Wednesday	Thursday	Friday	Saturday

Praise How does scripture describe God?

_____
_____
_____
_____
_____
_____
_____
_____
_____
_____
_____
_____
_____
_____
_____
_____
_____
_____
_____
_____
_____
_____
_____

Profess
What specific truth is God encouraging me to acknowledge?

_____
_____
_____
_____
_____
_____
_____
_____
_____
_____
_____
_____
_____
_____
_____

Pondering the Gospel or Grace Exchange

Requests
Make my requests known to God with praise and thanksgiving.

_____
_____
_____
_____
_____
_____
_____
_____
_____
_____
_____
_____
_____
_____
_____
_____
_____
_____
_____
_____
_____
_____
_____
_____
_____

Thanks
Give thanks to God, acknowledging His abundant grace in the midst of the situation, even when I don't understand.

_____
_____
_____
_____
_____
_____
_____
_____
_____
_____
_____
_____
_____
_____
_____
_____
_____
_____
_____
_____
_____
_____
_____
_____
_____

Week of _____ Daily Scripture Reading	Sunday	Monday	Tuesday
Wednesday	Thursday	Friday	Saturday

Praise How does scripture describe God?

Profess What specific truth is God encouraging me to acknowledge?

_____
_____
_____
_____
_____
_____
_____
_____
_____
_____
_____
_____
_____
_____
_____
_____

Pondering the Gospel or Grace Exchange

Requests

Make my requests known to God with praise and thanksgiving.

_____
_____
_____
_____
_____
_____
_____
_____
_____
_____
_____
_____
_____
_____
_____
_____
_____
_____
_____
_____
_____
_____
_____
_____
_____

Thanks

Give thanks to God, acknowledging His abundant grace in the midst of the situation, even when I don't understand.

_____
_____
_____
_____
_____
_____
_____
_____
_____
_____
_____
_____
_____
_____
_____
_____
_____
_____
_____
_____
_____
_____
_____
_____
_____

Week of _____ Daily Scripture Reading	Sunday	Monday	Tuesday
Wednesday	Thursday	Friday	Saturday

Praise How does scripture describe God?

_____
_____
_____
_____
_____
_____
_____
_____
_____
_____
_____
_____
_____
_____
_____
_____
_____
_____
_____
_____
_____
_____
_____
_____

Profess
What specific truth is God encouraging me to acknowledge?

_____
_____
_____
_____
_____
_____
_____
_____
_____
_____
_____
_____
_____
_____
_____
_____
_____

Pondering the Gospel or Grace Exchange

Requests

Make my requests known to God with praise and thanksgiving.

_____

Thanks

Give thanks to God, acknowledging His abundant grace in the midst of the situation, even when I don't understand.

_____

Week of _____ Daily Scripture Reading	Sunday	Monday	Tuesday
Wednesday	Thursday	Friday	Saturday

Praise How does scripture describe God?

_____
_____
_____
_____
_____
_____
_____
_____
_____
_____
_____
_____
_____
_____
_____
_____
_____
_____
_____
_____
_____
_____

Profess
What specific truth is God encouraging me to acknowledge?

_____
_____
_____
_____
_____
_____
_____
_____
_____
_____
_____
_____
_____
_____
_____
_____

Pondering the Gospel or Grace Exchange

Requests

Make my requests known to God with praise and thanksgiving.

_____

_____

_____

_____

_____

_____

_____

_____

_____

_____

_____

_____

_____

_____

_____

_____

_____

_____

_____

_____

_____

_____

_____

_____

_____

_____

Thanks

Give thanks to God, acknowledging His abundant grace in the midst of the situation, even when I don't understand.

_____

_____

_____

_____

_____

_____

_____

_____

_____

_____

_____

_____

_____

_____

_____

_____

_____

_____

_____

_____

_____

_____

_____

_____

_____

_____

Week of _____ Daily Scripture Reading	Sunday	Monday	Tuesday
Wednesday	Thursday	Friday	Saturday

Praise How does scripture describe God?

_____
_____
_____
_____
_____
_____
_____
_____
_____
_____
_____
_____
_____
_____
_____
_____
_____
_____
_____
_____
_____
_____

Profess
What specific truth is God encouraging me to acknowledge?

_____
_____
_____
_____
_____
_____
_____
_____
_____
_____
_____
_____
_____
_____
_____
_____

Pondering the Gospel or Grace Exchange

Requests

Make my requests known to God with praise and thanksgiving.

_____
_____
_____
_____
_____
_____
_____
_____
_____
_____
_____
_____
_____
_____
_____
_____
_____
_____
_____
_____
_____
_____
_____
_____
_____
_____

Thanks

Give thanks to God, acknowledging His abundant grace in the midst of the situation, even when I don't understand.

_____
_____
_____
_____
_____
_____
_____
_____
_____
_____
_____
_____
_____
_____
_____
_____
_____
_____
_____
_____
_____
_____
_____
_____
_____
_____

Week of _____ Daily Scripture Reading	Sunday	Monday	Tuesday
Wednesday	Thursday	Friday	Saturday

Praise How does scripture describe God?

_____
_____
_____
_____
_____
_____
_____
_____
_____
_____
_____
_____
_____
_____
_____
_____
_____
_____
_____
_____
_____
_____

Profess
What specific truth is God encouraging me to acknowledge?

_____
_____
_____
_____
_____
_____
_____
_____
_____
_____
_____
_____
_____
_____
_____
_____

Pondering the Gospel or Grace Exchange

Requests

Make my requests known to God with praise and thanksgiving.

_____
_____
_____
_____
_____
_____
_____
_____
_____
_____
_____
_____
_____
_____
_____
_____
_____
_____
_____
_____
_____
_____
_____
_____
_____
_____

Thanks

Give thanks to God, acknowledging His abundant grace in the midst of the situation, even when I don't understand.

_____
_____
_____
_____
_____
_____
_____
_____
_____
_____
_____
_____
_____
_____
_____
_____
_____
_____
_____
_____
_____
_____
_____
_____
_____
_____

Week of _____ Daily Scripture Reading	Sunday	Monday	Tuesday
Wednesday	Thursday	Friday	Saturday

Praise How does scripture describe God?

_____
_____
_____
_____
_____
_____
_____
_____
_____
_____
_____
_____
_____
_____
_____
_____
_____
_____
_____
_____
_____
_____
_____

Profess
What specific truth is God encouraging me to acknowledge?

_____
_____
_____
_____
_____
_____
_____
_____
_____
_____
_____
_____
_____
_____
_____
_____

Pondering the Gospel or Grace Exchange

Requests

Make my requests known to God with praise and thanksgiving.

_____
_____
_____
_____
_____
_____
_____
_____
_____
_____
_____
_____
_____
_____
_____
_____
_____
_____
_____
_____
_____
_____
_____
_____
_____
_____
_____

Thanks

Give thanks to God, acknowledging His abundant grace in the midst of the situation, even when I don't understand.

_____
_____
_____
_____
_____
_____
_____
_____
_____
_____
_____
_____
_____
_____
_____
_____
_____
_____
_____
_____
_____
_____
_____
_____
_____
_____
_____

Week of _____ Daily Scripture Reading	Sunday	Monday	Tuesday
Wednesday	Thursday	Friday	Saturday

Praise How does scripture describe God?

_____
_____
_____
_____
_____
_____
_____
_____
_____
_____
_____
_____
_____
_____
_____
_____
_____
_____
_____
_____
_____

Profess
What specific truth is God encouraging me to acknowledge?

___

Pondering the Gospel or Grace Exchange

Requests
Make my requests known to God with praise and thanksgiving.

_____

_____

_____

_____

_____

_____

_____

_____

_____

_____

_____

_____

_____

_____

_____

_____

_____

_____

_____

_____

_____

_____

_____

Thanks
Give thanks to God, acknowledging His abundant grace in the midst of the situation, even when I don't understand.

_____

_____

_____

_____

_____

_____

_____

_____

_____

_____

_____

_____

_____

_____

_____

_____

_____

_____

_____

_____

_____

_____

_____

Week of _____ Daily Scripture Reading	Sunday	Monday	Tuesday
Wednesday	Thursday	Friday	Saturday

Praise How does scripture describe God?

_____
_____
_____
_____
_____
_____
_____
_____
_____
_____
_____
_____
_____
_____
_____
_____
_____
_____
_____
_____
_____

Profess
What specific truth is God encouraging me to acknowledge?

Pondering the Gospel or Grace Exchange

Requests

Make my requests known to God with praise and thanksgiving.

Thanks

Give thanks to God, acknowledging His abundant grace in the midst of the situation, even when I don't understand.

Week of _____ Daily Scripture Reading	Sunday	Monday	Tuesday
Wednesday	Thursday	Friday	Saturday

Praise How does scripture describe God?

Profess What specific truth is God encouraging me to acknowledge?

_____
_____
_____
_____
_____
_____
_____
_____
_____
_____
_____
_____
_____
_____
_____
_____

Pondering the Gospel or Grace Exchange

Requests

Make my requests known to God with praise and thanksgiving.

_____
_____
_____
_____
_____
_____
_____
_____
_____
_____
_____
_____
_____
_____
_____
_____
_____
_____
_____
_____
_____
_____
_____
_____
_____
_____
_____

Thanks

Give thanks to God, acknowledging His abundant grace in the midst of the situation, even when I don't understand.

_____
_____
_____
_____
_____
_____
_____
_____
_____
_____
_____
_____
_____
_____
_____
_____
_____
_____
_____
_____
_____
_____
_____
_____
_____
_____
_____

Week of _____ Daily Scripture Reading	Sunday	Monday	Tuesday
Wednesday	Thursday	Friday	Saturday

Praise How does scripture describe God?

_____
_____
_____
_____
_____
_____
_____
_____
_____
_____
_____
_____
_____
_____
_____
_____
_____
_____
_____
_____
_____
_____
_____
_____
_____

Profess What specific truth is God encouraging me to acknowledge?

_____
_____
_____
_____
_____
_____
_____
_____
_____
_____
_____
_____
_____
_____
_____

Pondering the Gospel or Grace Exchange

Requests

Make my requests known to God with praise and thanksgiving.

_____
_____
_____
_____
_____
_____
_____
_____
_____
_____
_____
_____
_____
_____
_____
_____
_____
_____
_____
_____
_____
_____
_____
_____

Thanks

Give thanks to God, acknowledging His abundant grace in the midst of the situation, even when I don't understand.

_____
_____
_____
_____
_____
_____
_____
_____
_____
_____
_____
_____
_____
_____
_____
_____
_____
_____
_____
_____
_____
_____
_____
_____

Week of _____ Daily Scripture Reading	Sunday	Monday	Tuesday
Wednesday	Thursday	Friday	Saturday

Praise How does scripture describe God?

_____
_____
_____
_____
_____
_____
_____
_____
_____
_____
_____
_____
_____
_____
_____
_____
_____
_____
_____
_____
_____
_____
_____

Profess
What specific truth is God encouraging me to acknowledge?

_____
_____
_____
_____
_____
_____
_____
_____
_____
_____
_____
_____
_____
_____
_____

Pondering the Gospel or Grace Exchange

Requests

Make my requests known to God with praise and thanksgiving.

_____
_____
_____
_____
_____
_____
_____
_____
_____
_____
_____
_____
_____
_____
_____
_____
_____
_____
_____
_____
_____
_____
_____
_____
_____
_____
_____

Thanks

Give thanks to God, acknowledging His abundant grace in the midst of the situation, even when I don't understand.

_____
_____
_____
_____
_____
_____
_____
_____
_____
_____
_____
_____
_____
_____
_____
_____
_____
_____
_____
_____
_____
_____
_____
_____
_____
_____
_____

Week of _____ Daily Scripture Reading	Sunday	Monday	Tuesday
Wednesday	Thursday	Friday	Saturday

Praise How does scripture describe God?

_____
_____
_____
_____
_____
_____
_____
_____
_____
_____
_____
_____
_____
_____
_____
_____
_____
_____
_____
_____
_____
_____

Profess
What specific truth is God encouraging me to acknowledge?

_____
_____
_____
_____
_____
_____
_____
_____
_____
_____
_____
_____
_____
_____
_____

Pondering the Gospel or Grace Exchange

Requests

Make my requests known to God with praise and thanksgiving.

_____
_____
_____
_____
_____
_____
_____
_____
_____
_____
_____
_____
_____
_____
_____
_____
_____
_____
_____
_____
_____
_____
_____
_____
_____
_____

Thanks

Give thanks to God, acknowledging His abundant grace in the midst of the situation, even when I don't understand.

_____
_____
_____
_____
_____
_____
_____
_____
_____
_____
_____
_____
_____
_____
_____
_____
_____
_____
_____
_____
_____
_____
_____
_____
_____
_____

Week of _____ Daily Scripture Reading	Sunday	Monday	Tuesday
Wednesday	Thursday	Friday	Saturday

Praise How does scripture describe God?

_____
_____
_____
_____
_____
_____
_____
_____
_____
_____
_____
_____
_____
_____
_____
_____
_____
_____
_____
_____
_____
_____
_____

Profess
What specific truth is God encouraging me to acknowledge?

_____
_____
_____
_____
_____
_____
_____
_____
_____
_____
_____
_____
_____
_____

Pondering the Gospel or Grace Exchange

Requests
Make my requests known to God with praise and thanksgiving.

_____
_____
_____
_____
_____
_____
_____
_____
_____
_____
_____
_____
_____
_____
_____
_____
_____
_____
_____
_____
_____
_____
_____
_____
_____
_____
_____
_____

Thanks
Give thanks to God, acknowledging His abundant grace in the midst of the situation, even when I don't understand.

_____
_____
_____
_____
_____
_____
_____
_____
_____
_____
_____
_____
_____
_____
_____
_____
_____
_____
_____
_____
_____
_____
_____
_____
_____
_____
_____
_____

Week of	Sunday	Monday	Tuesday
Daily Scripture Reading			
Wednesday	Thursday	Friday	Saturday

Praise How does scripture describe God?

Profess
What specific truth is God encouraging me to acknowledge?

_____
_____
_____
_____
_____
_____
_____
_____
_____
_____
_____
_____
_____
_____
_____
_____

Pondering the Gospel or Grace Exchange

Requests

Make my requests known to God with praise and thanksgiving.

_____
_____
_____
_____
_____
_____
_____
_____
_____
_____
_____
_____
_____
_____
_____
_____
_____
_____
_____
_____
_____
_____
_____

Thanks

Give thanks to God, acknowledging His abundant grace in the midst of the situation, even when I don't understand.

_____
_____
_____
_____
_____
_____
_____
_____
_____
_____
_____
_____
_____
_____
_____
_____
_____
_____
_____
_____
_____
_____
_____

Week of _____ Daily Scripture Reading	Sunday	Monday	Tuesday
Wednesday	Thursday	Friday	Saturday

Praise How does scripture describe God?

_____
_____
_____
_____
_____
_____
_____
_____
_____
_____
_____
_____
_____
_____
_____
_____
_____
_____
_____
_____
_____

Profess
What specific truth is God encouraging me to acknowledge?

_____
_____
_____
_____
_____
_____
_____
_____
_____
_____
_____
_____
_____
_____
_____

Pondering the Gospel or Grace Exchange

Requests
Make my requests known to God with praise and thanksgiving.

_____
_____
_____
_____
_____
_____
_____
_____
_____
_____
_____
_____
_____
_____
_____
_____
_____
_____
_____
_____
_____
_____
_____
_____
_____
_____
_____

Thanks
Give thanks to God, acknowledging His abundant grace in the midst of the situation, even when I don't understand.

_____
_____
_____
_____
_____
_____
_____
_____
_____
_____
_____
_____
_____
_____
_____
_____
_____
_____
_____
_____
_____
_____
_____
_____
_____
_____
_____

Week of _____ Daily Scripture Reading	Sunday	Monday	Tuesday
Wednesday	Thursday	Friday	Saturday

Praise How does scripture describe God?

_____
_____
_____
_____
_____
_____
_____
_____
_____
_____
_____
_____
_____
_____
_____
_____
_____
_____
_____

Profess
What specific truth is God encouraging me to acknowledge?

_____
_____
_____
_____
_____
_____
_____
_____
_____
_____
_____
_____
_____
_____
_____
_____
_____

Pondering the Gospel or Grace Exchange

Requests

Make my requests known to God with praise and thanksgiving.

_____
_____
_____
_____
_____
_____
_____
_____
_____
_____
_____
_____
_____
_____
_____
_____
_____
_____
_____
_____
_____
_____
_____
_____
_____

Thanks

Give thanks to God, acknowledging His abundant grace in the midst of the situation, even when I don't understand.

_____
_____
_____
_____
_____
_____
_____
_____
_____
_____
_____
_____
_____
_____
_____
_____
_____
_____
_____
_____
_____
_____
_____
_____
_____

Week of _____ Daily Scripture Reading	Sunday	Monday	Tuesday
Wednesday	Thursday	Friday	Saturday

Praise How does scripture describe God?

_____
_____
_____
_____
_____
_____
_____
_____
_____
_____
_____
_____
_____
_____
_____
_____
_____
_____
_____
_____
_____

Profess
What specific truth is God encouraging me to acknowledge?

___

Pondering the Gospel or Grace Exchange

Requests

Make my requests known to God with praise and thanksgiving.

_____
_____
_____
_____
_____
_____
_____
_____
_____
_____
_____
_____
_____
_____
_____
_____
_____
_____
_____
_____
_____
_____
_____
_____
_____
_____
_____
_____

Thanks

Give thanks to God, acknowledging His abundant grace in the midst of the situation, even when I don't understand.

_____
_____
_____
_____
_____
_____
_____
_____
_____
_____
_____
_____
_____
_____
_____
_____
_____
_____
_____
_____
_____
_____
_____
_____
_____
_____
_____

Week of _____ Daily Scripture Reading	Sunday	Monday	Tuesday
Wednesday	Thursday	Friday	Saturday

Praise How does scripture describe God?

_____
_____
_____
_____
_____
_____
_____
_____
_____
_____
_____
_____
_____
_____
_____
_____
_____
_____
_____
_____
_____
_____

Profess What specific truth is God encouraging me to acknowledge?

_____
_____
_____
_____
_____
_____
_____
_____
_____
_____
_____
_____
_____
_____
_____
_____

Pondering the Gospel or Grace Exchange

Requests

Make my requests known to God with praise and thanksgiving.

_____
_____
_____
_____
_____
_____
_____
_____
_____
_____
_____
_____
_____
_____
_____
_____
_____
_____
_____
_____
_____
_____
_____
_____
_____
_____
_____
_____

Thanks

Give thanks to God, acknowledging His abundant grace in the midst of the situation, even when I don't understand.

_____
_____
_____
_____
_____
_____
_____
_____
_____
_____
_____
_____
_____
_____
_____
_____
_____
_____
_____
_____
_____
_____
_____
_____
_____
_____
_____
_____

Week of _____ Daily Scripture Reading	Sunday	Monday	Tuesday
Wednesday	Thursday	Friday	Saturday

Praise How does scripture describe God?

Profess
What specific truth is God encouraging me to acknowledge?

_____
_____
_____
_____
_____
_____
_____
_____
_____
_____
_____
_____
_____
_____
_____

Pondering the Gospel or Grace Exchange

Requests

Make my requests known to God with praise and thanksgiving.

_____
_____
_____
_____
_____
_____
_____
_____
_____
_____
_____
_____
_____
_____
_____
_____
_____
_____
_____
_____
_____
_____
_____
_____
_____

Thanks

Give thanks to God, acknowledging His abundant grace in the midst of the situation, even when I don't understand.

_____
_____
_____
_____
_____
_____
_____
_____
_____
_____
_____
_____
_____
_____
_____
_____
_____
_____
_____
_____
_____
_____
_____
_____
_____

Peace Through the Grace Exchange

"Beloved, do not be surprised at the fiery ordeal among you, which comes upon you for your testing, as though some strange thing were happening to you; but to the degree that you share the sufferings of Christ, keep on rejoicing; so that also at the revelation of His glory, you may rejoice with exultation."
1 Peter 4:12-13

Using the **Grace Exchange**

1. As we read Scripture, God will point out thoughts and behaviors that do not agree with His truth. Recognizing these patterns is the first step toward having our lives transformed by God. This process is what the Bible refers to as "sanctification" or being "conformed to the image of His Son" (Romans 8:29).

2. As we become aware of a pattern of sin (e.g. anxiety, overeating, fear, anger, pride), write it in the blocks on the "Give God" side. As we ask God to continue to show us our wrong thinking and misdirected desires that fuel our sin, He will show us what to write. Over time, as we read His word our recognition of our need for the gospel will grow.

3. In the "Receive from God" blocks, write the corresponding truth about God's character that we need God to exchange for us. (Include Scripture references.)

4. The cross in between the two sets of blocks reminds us that the "grace exchange" is only made possible by the gospel. We have been set free from the entanglement of sin by Christ's sacrifice on the cross. Because He was raised from the dead, we have access to the resurrection power that enables us to walk in truth. We have the Spirit in us, who intercedes for us and leads and guides us.

5. We can prayerfully use this section to renew our mind. During the day, we can continue to ask God to show us areas of weakness to keep exchanging for His grace. Sanctification is a moment by moment process. Beginning the day with renewing our mind does not ensure godly thoughts and behaviors all day, but simply sets us up to better recognize and deal with ungodly desires and wrong motives as we encounter them. Then, as we repent, we need to remember that we cannot and should not do it in our own strength, but instead ask God to do this work in us and to grow us in relying on His Spirit to work in us.

the Grace Exchange

Give God...
Patterns of self-sufficiency, pride, self-salvation strategies

MY Weakness / Pride / Sin

Christ died so that I would be FREE from...

While I was still weak and a sinner, at the right time, Christ died for me. Romans 5:6-8

I am feeble and weak in my prayers. I don't know how to pray.

Worry and Anxiety I am worried and bothered about so many things. Luke 10:41

Efficiency, Organization, and Perfection Worshiping these to keep from feeling like a failure

---

"Lay aside the old self, which is being corrupted in accordance with the lusts of deceit, ... be renewed in the spirit of your mind, and put on the new self, which in the likeness of God has been created in righteousness and holiness of truth."
Ephesians 4:22-24

Receive from God...
God's character, His thoughts,
His power for change

I have hope and am not put to shame – God's love has been poured into my heart by the Holy Spirit. Romans 5:5

The Holy Spirit helps my weakness.
He intercedes for me.
He knows God's mind.
Romans 8:26-27

Cause me to cast all my anxiety on You because You will take care of me!
1 Peter 5:7

You alone God are worthy of worship.
Cause me to trust
Your GRACE
Your TRUTH

"And He said to me, My grace is sufficient for you, for power is perfected in weakness."
2 Corinthians 12:9

the Grace Exchange

Give God...
Patterns of self-sufficiency, pride, self-salvation strategies

MY Weakness Pride Sin

Christ died so that I would be FREE from...

"... do not be conformed to this world, but be transformed by the renewing of your mind, that you may prove what the will of God is, that which is good and acceptable and perfect."
Romans 12:2

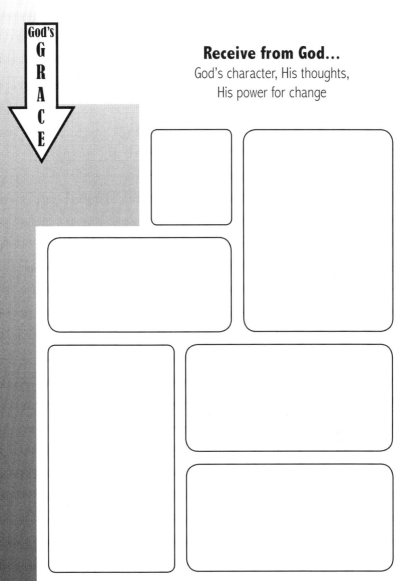

Receive from God...
God's character, His thoughts,
His power for change

God's GRACE

""And God is able to make all grace abound to you, so that in all things at all times, having all that you need, you will abound in every good work."
2 Corinthians 9:8

the **Grace Exchange**

Give God...
Patterns of self-sufficiency, pride, self-salvation strategies

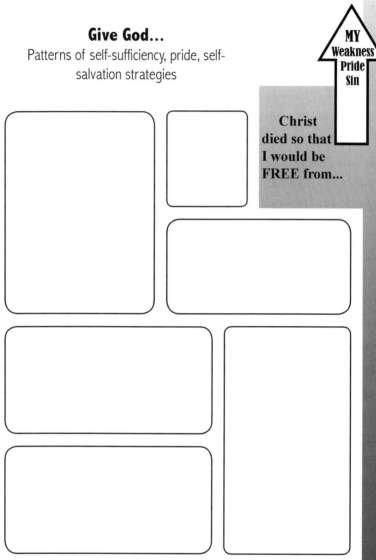

"Lay aside the old self, which is being corrupted in accordance with the lusts of deceit, ... be renewed in the spirit of your mind, and put on the new self, which in the likeness of God has been created in righteousness and holiness of truth."
Ephesians 4:22-24

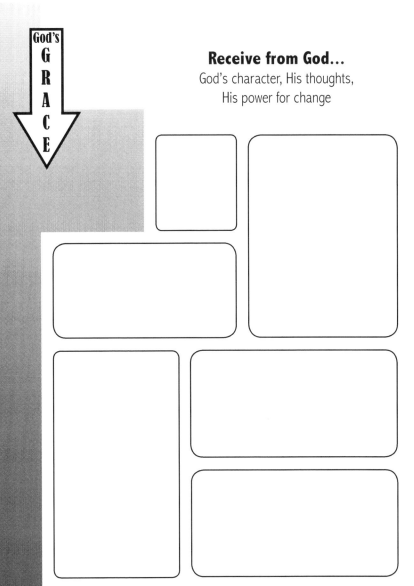

God's GRACE

Receive from God...
God's character, His thoughts,
His power for change

""And God is able to make all grace abound to you, so that in all things at all times, having all that you need, you will abound in every good work."
2 Corinthians 9:8

the **Grace Exchange**

Give God...
Patterns of self-sufficiency, pride, self-salvation strategies

"... do not be conformed to this world, but be transformed by the renewing of your mind, that you may prove what the will of God is, that which is good and acceptable and perfect."
Romans 12:2

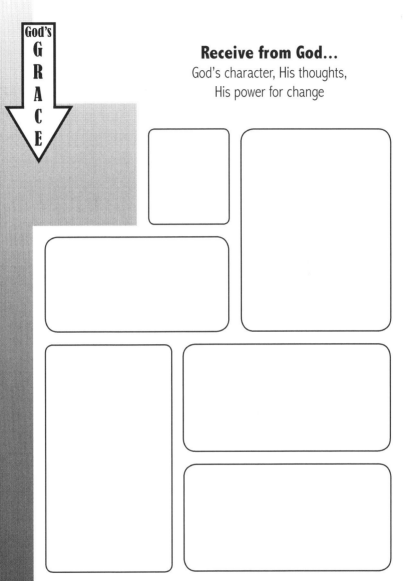

Receive from God…
God's character, His thoughts,
His power for change

God's
G
R
A
C
E

""And God is able to make all grace abound to you, so that in all things at all times, having all that you need, you will abound in every good work."
2 Corinthians 9:8

the Grace Exchange

Give God...
Patterns of self-sufficiency, pride, self-salvation strategies

MY Weakness Pride Sin

Christ died so that I would be FREE from...

"... do not be conformed to this world, but be transformed by the renewing of your mind, that you may prove what the will of God is, that which is good and acceptable and perfect."
Romans 12:2

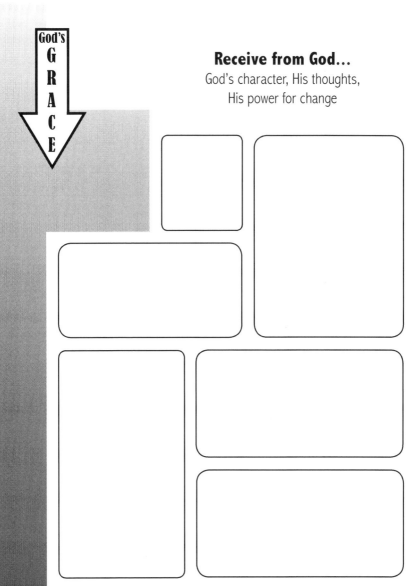

God's GRACE

Receive from God...
God's character, His thoughts,
His power for change

""And God is able to make all grace abound to you, so that in all things at all times, having all that you need, you will abound in every good work."
2 Corinthians 9:8

the Grace Exchange

Give God...
Patterns of self-sufficiency, pride, self-salvation strategies

"Lay aside the old self, which is being corrupted in accordance with the lusts of deceit, ... be renewed in the spirit of your mind, and put on the new self, which in the likeness of God has been created in righteousness and holiness of truth."
Ephesians 4:22-24

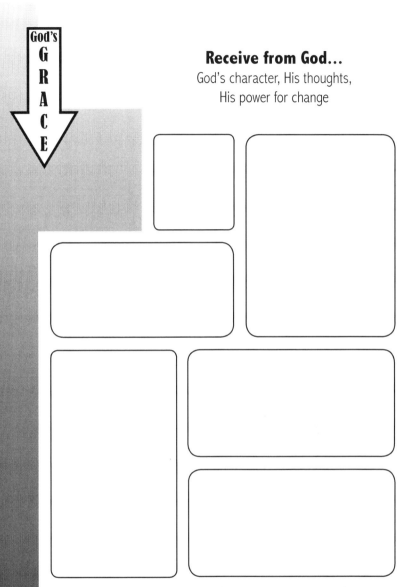

Receive from God...
God's character, His thoughts,
His power for change

""And God is able to make all grace abound to you, so that in all things at all times, having all that you need, you will abound in every good work."
2 Corinthians 9:8

the Grace Exchange

Give God...
Patterns of self-sufficiency, pride, self-salvation strategies

"... do not be conformed to this world, but be transformed by the renewing of your mind, that you may prove what the will of God is, that which is good and acceptable and perfect."
Romans 12:2

God's GRACE

Receive from God...
God's character, His thoughts,
His power for change

""And God is able to make all grace abound to you, so that in all things at all times, having all that you need, you will abound in every good work."
2 Corinthians 9:8

Using the **What Do I Believe?** chart:

Peace, or lack of it, is a good indicator of what we believe about God and who or what we are worshipping in that moment. When our heart is aligned to value what God values and is in step with the truth of God's Word, we will experience the peace of God in our lives (Isaiah 26:3, Philippians 4:7). A lack of peace makes us aware something is amiss, and that the intentions and desires of our heart are not in concert with His. If what we believe or trust is in line with worldly wisdom and our own selfish desires, the result is anxiety (Philippians 4:6-7), a fearful and troubled heart (John 14:1, 27), despair (Psalm 42:5, 11), anger (James 1:19-20) and other sin.

Adversity, trials, mundane events, problems, pain - As the events of our lives play out, we have an inward reaction to each of them. Even the most mundane event has correlating initial thoughts and emotions, such as restlessness or boredom. Happy events can trigger excitement, joy or even suspicion that it will not last. Usually, we are not even aware of our corresponding thoughts, desires or fears. We are even less aware of what our reactions reveal about what we believe about God. It often takes painful circumstances to bring us to that level of consciousness, so it is generally pain that God uses to make us aware of what is going on in our heart. Pain is designed to move us toward God and allow His purifying process to do the work of transforming our hearts and minds. God uses trials and adversity to expose underlying wrong thinking and selfish and inordinate desires of the heart (James 2; 4:1-4) in order to reorient our hearts and lives more fully and to consistently worship him (Hebrews 12:3-11) and thus to experience life abundantly (John 10:10). The process of recognizing our areas of unbelief or lack of trust in God can be excruciating because we have spent much of our lives rationalizing, denying, avoiding, minimizing or justifying our thoughts, emotions and behaviors. Let's ask God to enable us to embrace the pain instead of running from or ignoring it.

Initial thoughts and emotions - God designed us with emotions because He created man in His own image, and He has emotions. Because of the fall, our emotions are not pure like His are. They are intertwined with deception and depravity. The question is what am I going to do with these emotions? Am I going to let them determine my actions or am I going to filter my emotions through the truth of the gospel in order to come in line with who God is according to His Word? The only way to do that is to recognize that I cannot change how I feel, only Christ can.

Picture of the cross (on chart) - Jesus paid in full on the cross for the destruction, delusion and depravity of our wrong desires. As we humbly acknowledge His forgiveness we can then receive His power (grace) to experience our emotions in pure form and to think in line with His thoughts, reflecting His true character.

What Do I Believe?

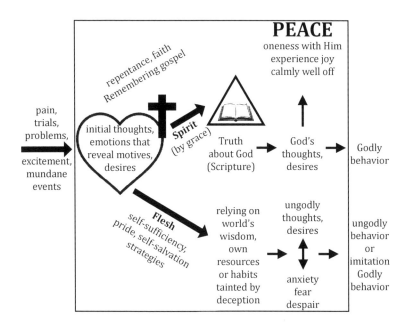

All three must be present in order to have Biblical belief, trust or faith.
    1) I KNOW who God is (from Scripture)
    2) I AGREE with what He says about Himself
    3) my MOTIVATIONS/ THOUGHTS/ ACTIONS agree with that truth

(If we think we believe or trust God in an area, we can look to see if our motives, thoughts and actions confirm that.)

"For since, in the wisdom of God, the world did not know God through wisdom."
    1 Corinthians 1:21

This Read through the Bible in a Year plan has been developed to go along with Gospel Journey, giving the opportunity to read through the Bible in community.

Using this reading schedule gives you the opportunity to read both the Old Testament and the New Testament together in chronological order. With the exception of Sundays, you will be reading around three chapters a day – two in the Old Testament and one in the New Testament for most of the year*. Each Sunday you will read three Psalms and one chapter of one of the other poetry books. If you plan to use this schedule write the chapters in the corresponding calendar boxes at the beginning of each week in the front section.

Your Gospel Journey gives you a place to write down what you learn about God as you are reading. This enables you to remember what you saw about God and to praise Him during the week. If you write one thing down each day in your "Praise" column, at the end of the year you will have 365 ways to praise God. The "Profess" page gives you a place to record the ways God is calling you to grow by His grace in trusting Him and in believing the gospel as the means to that grace.

*A special encouragement. If you get behind in reading, don't try to catch up. Always read what is set for that day. If you miss some chapters you can read them next year when you read through again. We have found that one of the benefits of reading the same Bible schedule as others in your community of believers is that it offers encouragement and accountability to be in the Word, and gives opportunity to discuss the things God presses on your heart.

There are many different reading plans available for reading Scripture. Feel free to use another if you have one you like better.

Read through the Bible in a Year

Week One
Psalms 1-3, Prov. 1
Genesis 1-2, Matt. 1
Genesis 3-4, Matt. 2
Genesis 5-6, Matt. 3
Genesis 7-8, Matt. 4
Genesis 9-10, Matt. 5
Genesis 11-12, Matt. 6

Week Two
Psalms 4-7, Prov. 2
Genesis 13-14, Matt. 7
Genesis 15-16, Matt. 8
Genesis 17-18, Matt. 9
Genesis 19-20, Matt. 10
Genesis 21-22, Matt. 11
Genesis 23-24, Matt. 12

Week Three
Psalms 8-11, Prov. 3
Job 1-2, Matt. 13
Job 3-4, Matt. 14
Job 5-6, Matt. 15
Job 7-8, Matt. 16
Job 9-10, Matt. 17
Job 11-12, Matt. 18

Week Four
Psalms 12-14, Prov. 4
Job 13-14, Matt. 19
Job 15-16, Matt. 20
Job 17-18, Matt. 21
Job 19-20, Matt. 22
Job 21-22, Matt. 23
Job 23-24, Matt. 24

Week Five
Psalms 15-17, Prov. 5
Job 25-26, Matt. 25
Job 27-28, Matt. 26
Job 29-30, Matt. 27
Job 31-32, Matt. 28
Job 32-34, Mark 1
Job 35-36, Mark 2

Week Six
Psalms 18-20, Prov. 6
Job 37-38, Mark 3
Job 39-40, Mark 4
Job 41-42, Mark 5
Genesis 25-26, Mark 6
Genesis 27-28, Mark 7
Genesis 29-30, Mark 8

Week Seven
Psalms 21-23, Prov. 7
Genesis 31-32, Mark 9
Genesis 33-34, Mk. 10
Genesis 35-36, Mk. 11
Genesis 37-38, Mk. 12
Genesis 39-40, Mk. 13
Genesis 41-42, Mk. 14

Week Eight
Psalms 24-26, Prov. 8
Genesis 43-44, Mk. 15
Genesis 45-46, Mk. 16
Genesis 47-48, Luke 1
Genesis 49-50, Luke 2
Exodus 1-2, Luke 3
Exodus 3-4, Luke 4

Week Nine
Psalms 27-29, Prov. 9
Exodus 5-6, Luke 5
Exodus 7-8, Luke 6
Exodus 9-10, Luke 7
Exodus 11-12, Luke 8
Exodus 13-14, Luke 9
Exodus 15-16, Luke 10

Week Ten
Psalms 30-32, Prov. 10
Exodus 17-18, Luke 11
Exodus 19-20, Luke 12
Exodus 21-22, Luke 13
Exodus 23-24, Luke 14
Exodus 25-26, Luke 15
Exodus 27-28, Luke 16

Week Eleven
Psalms 33-35, Prov. 11
Exodus 29-30, Luke 17
Exodus 31-32, Luke 18
Exodus 33-34, Luke 19
Exodus 35-36, Luke 20
Exodus 37-38, Luke 21
Exodus 39-40, Luke 22

Week Twelve
Psalms 36-38, Prov.12
Leviticus 1-2, Luke 23
Leviticus 3-4, Luke 24
Leviticus 5-6, John 1
Leviticus 7-8, John 2
Leviticus 9-10, John 3
Leviticus 11-12, John 4

Week Thirteen
Psalms 39-41, Prov. 13
Leviticus 13-14, John 5
Leviticus 15-16, John 6
Leviticus 17-18, John 7
Leviticus 19-20, John 8
Leviticus 21-22, John 9
Leviticus 23-24, John 10

Week Fourteen
Psalms 42-44, Prov. 14
Leviticus 25-27,John 11
Numbers 1-2, John 12
Numbers 3-4, John 13
Numbers 5-6, John 14
Numbers 7-8, John 15
Numbers 9-10, John 16

Week Fifteen
Psalms 45-47, Prov. 15
Numbers 11-12, John 17
Numbers 13-14, John 18
Numbers 15-16, John 19
Numbers 17-18, John 20
Numbers 19-20, John 21
Numbers 21-22, Acts 1

Week Sixteen
Psalms 48-50, Prov. 16
Numbers 23-24, Acts 2
Numbers 25-26, Acts 3
Numbers 27-28, Acts 4
Numbers 29-30, Acts5
Numbers 31-32, Acts 6
Numbers 33-34, Acts 7

Week Seventeen
Psalms 51-53, Prov. 17
Numbers 35-36, Acts 8
Deut. 1-2, Acts 9
Deut. 3-4, Acts 10
Deut. 5-6, Acts 11
Deut. 7-8, Acts 12
Deut. 9-10, Acts 13

Week Eighteen
Psalms 54-56, Prov. 18
Deut. 11-12, Acts 14
Deut. 13-14, Gal. 1
Deut. 15-16, Gal. 2
Deut. 17-18, Gal. 3
Deut. 19-20, Gal. 4
Deut. 21-22, Gal. 5

Week Nineteen
Psalms 57-59, Prov. 19
Deut. 23-24, Gal. 6
Deut. 25-26, James 1
Deut. 27-28, James 2
Deut. 29-30, James 3
Deut. 31-32, James 4
Deut. 33-34, James 5

Week Twenty
Psalms 60-62, Prov. 20
Joshua 1-2, Acts 15-17
Joshua 3-4, Phil. 1
Joshua 5-6, Phil. 2
Joshua 7-8, Phil. 3
Joshua 9-10, Phil. 4
Joshua 11-12, 1 Thes. 1

Week Twenty-one
Psalms 63-65, Prov. 21
Joshua 13-14, 1 Thes. 2
Joshua 15-16, 1 Thes. 3
Joshua 17-18, 1 Thes. 4
Joshua 19-20, 1 Thes. 5
Joshua 21-22, 2 Thes. 1
Joshua 23-24, 2 Thes. 2

Week Twenty-two
Psalms 66-68, Prov. 22
Judges 1-2, 2 Thes. 3
Judges 3-4, 1 Cor. 1
Judges 5-6, 1 Cor. 2
Judges 7-8, 1 Cor. 3
Judges 9-10, 1 Cor.4
Judges 11-12, 1 Cor. 5

Week Twenty-three
Psalms 69-71, Prov. 23
Ruth 1-2, 1 Cor. 6
Ruth 3-4, 1 Cor. 7
Judges 13-14, 1 Cor. 8
Judges 15-16, 1 Cor. 9
Judges 17-18, 1 Cor.10
Judges 19-21 Cor. 11

Week Twenty-four
Psalms 72-74, Prov. 24
I Samuel 1-2, 1 Cor. 12
I Samuel 3-4, 1 Cor. 13
I Samuel 5-6, 1 Cor. 14
I Samuel 7-8, 1 Cor. 15
I Sam. 9-10, 1 Cor. 16
I Sam. 11-12, 2 Cor. 1

Week Twenty-five
Psalms 75-77, Prov. 25
I Sam. 13-14, 2 Cor. 2
I Sam. 15-16, 2 Cor. 3
I Sam. 17-18, 2 Cor. 4
I Sam. 19-20, 2 Cor. 5
I Sam. 21-22, 2 Cor. 6
1 Sam. 23-24, 2 Cor. 7

Week Twenty-six
Psalms 78-80, Prov. 26
I Sam. 25-26, 2 Cor. 8
I Sam. 27-28, 2 Cor. 9
I Sam. 29-31, 2 Cor. 10
2 Sam. 1-2, 2 Cor. 11
2 Sam. 3-4, 2 Cor. 12
2 Sam. 5-6, 2 Cor. 13

Week Twenty-seven
Psalms 81-83, Prov. 27
2 Sam. 7-8, Acts 18
2 Sam. 9-10, Acts 19
2 Sam. 11-12, Eph. 1
2 Sam. 13-14, Eph. 2
2 Sam. 15-16, Eph. 3
2 Sam. 17-18, Eph. 4

Week Twenty-eight
Psalms 84-86, Prov. 28
2 Sam. 19-20, Eph. 5
2 Sam. 21-22, Eph. 6
2 Sam. 23-24, Rom. 1
1 Kings 1-2, Rom. 2
1 Kings 3-4, Rom. 3
1 Kings 5-6, Rom. 4

Week Twenty-nine
Psalms 87-90, Prov. 29
1 Kings 7-8, Rom. 5
1 Kings 9-10, Rom. 6
1 Kings 11-12, Rom. 7
1 Kings 13-14, Rom. 8
1 Kings 15-16, Rom. 9
1 Kings 17-18, Rom. 10

Week Thirty
Psalms 91-93, Prov. 30
1 Kings 19-20, Rom. 11
1 Kings 21-22, Rom. 12
2 Kings 1-2, Rom. 13
2 Kings 3-4, Rom. 14
2 Kings 5-6, Rom. 15
2 Kings 7-8, Rom. 16

Week Thirty-one
Psalms 94-96, Prov. 31
2 Kings 9-10, Acts 20
2 Kings 11-12, Acts 21
2 Kings 13-14, Acts 22
2 Kings 15-16, Acts 23
2 Kings 17-18, Acts 24
2 Kings 19-20, Acts 25

Week Thirty-two
Psalms 97-99, S.O.S. 1
2 Kings 21-22, Acts 26
2 Kings 23-24, Acts 27
1 Chron. 1-2, Acts 28
1 Chron. 3-4, Col. 1
1 Chron. 5-6, Col. 2
1 Chron. 7-8, Col. 3

Week Thirty-three
Ps. 100-102, S.O.S 2
1 Chron. 9-10, Col. 4
1 Chron. 11-12, Heb. 1
1 Chron. 13-14, Heb. 2
1 Chron. 15-16, Heb. 3
1 Chron. 17-18, Heb. 4
1 Chron. 19-20, Heb. 5

Week Thirty-four
Ps. 103-105, S.O.S. 3
1 Chron. 21-22, Heb. 6
1 Chron. 23-24, Heb. 7
1 Chron. 25-26, Heb. 8
1 Chron. 27-29, Heb. 9
2 Chron. 1-2, Heb. 10
2 Chron. 3-4, Heb. 11

Week Thirty-five
Ps. 106-108, S.O.S.4
2 Chron.5-6, Heb. 12
2 Chron. 7-8, Heb. 13
2 Chron. 9-10, Titus 1
2 Chron. 11-12, Titus 2
2 Chron. 13-14, Titus 3
2 Chron. 15-16, Philemon

Week Thirty-six
Ps. 109-111, S.O.S. 5
2 Chron. 17-18, 1 Tim. 1
2 Chron. 19-20, 1 Tim. 2
Joel 1-3, 1 Tim. 3
Obadiah, 1 Tim 4
Jonah 1-2, 1 Tim. 5
Jonah 3-4, 1 Tim. 6

Week Thirty-seven
Ps. 112-114, S.O.S. 6
2 Chron.21-22, 2 Tim.1
2 Chron.23-24, 2 Tim.2
2 Chron.25-26, 2 Tim.3
Amos 1-2, 2 Tim. 4
Amos 3-4, 1 Peter 1
Amos 5-6, 1 Peter 2

Week Thirty-eight
Amos 7-9, 1 Peter 3
2 Chron.27-28, 1 Peter 4
Hosea 1-2, 1 Peter 5
Hosea 3-4, 2 Peter 1
Ps. 115-118, S.O.S. 7
Hosea 5-6, 2 Peter 2
Hosea 7-8, 2 Peter 3

Week Thirty-nine
Ps. 119:1-40, S.O.S. 8
Hosea 9-10, 1 John 1
Hosea 11-12, 1 John 2
Hosea 13-14, 1 John 3
2 Chron. 29-31, 1 John 4
Isaiah 1-2, 1 John 5
Isaiah 3-4, 2 & 3 John

Week forty
Ps. 119:41-88, Ecc. 1
Isaiah 5-6, Jude
Isaiah 7-8, Rev. 1
Isaiah 9-10, Rev. 2
Isaiah 11-12, Rev. 3
Isaiah 13-14, Rev. 4
Isaiah 15-16, Rev. 5

Week forty-one
Ps. 119: 89-136, Ecc. 2
Isaiah 17-18, Rev. 6
Isaiah 19-20, Rev. 7
Isaiah 21-22, Rev. 8
Isaiah 23-24, Rev. 9
Isaiah 25-26, Rev. 10
Isaiah 27-28, Rev. 11

Week forty-two
Ps. 119: 137-176, Ecc. 3
Isaiah 29-30, Rev. 12
Isaiah 31-32, Rev. 13
Isaiah 33-34, Rev. 14
Isaiah 35-36, Rev. 15
Isaiah 37-38, Rev. 16
Isaiah 39-40, Rev. 17

Week forty-three
Ps. 120-122, Ecc. 4
Isaiah 41-43, Rev. 18
Isaiah 44-46, Rev. 19
Isaiah 47-49, Rev. 20
Isaiah 50-52, Rev. 21
Isaiah 53-55, Rev. 22
Isaiah 56-58

Week forty-four
Ps. 123-125, Ecc. 5
Isaiah 59-61
Isaiah 62-64
Isaiah 65-66
Micah 1-4
Micah 5-7
2 Chron 32-36

Week forty-five
Ps. 126-128, Ecc. 6
Nahum
Zephaniah
Habakkuk
Jeremiah 1-3
Jeremiah 4-6
Jeremiah 11-12, 26

Week forty-six
Ps. 129-131, Ecc. 7
Jeremiah 7-9
Jeremiah 10, 14-15
Jeremiah 16-18
Jeremiah 19-20, 35
Jeremiah 25, 36, 45
Jeremiah 46-49

Week forty-seven
Ps. 132-134, Ecc. 8
Jeremiah 13, 22-23
Jeremiah 24, 27-28
Jeremiah 29, 50-51
Jeremiah 30-33
Jeremiah 21,34,37
Jeremiah 38-39,52

Week forty-eight
Ps. 135-137, Ecc. 9
Jeremiah 40-42
Jeremiah 43-44, Lamentations
Daniel 1-3
Daniel 4-6
Daniel 7-9
Daniel 10-12

Week forty-nine
Ps. 138-140, Ecc.10
Ezekiel 1-4
Ezekiel 5-8
Ezekiel 9-12
Ezekiel 13-16
Ezekiel 17-20
Ezekiel 21-24

Week fifty
Ps. 141-143, Ecc. 11
Ezekiel 25-28
Ezekiel 29-32
Ezekiel 33-36
Ezekiel 37-40
Ezekiel 41-44
Ezekiel 45-48

Week fifty-one
Ps. 144-146, Ecc.12
Ezra 1-3
Ezra 4-6
Haggai
Zechariah 1-4
Zechariah 5-8
Esther 1-5

Week Fifty-two
Esther 6-10
Ezra 7-10
Nehemiah 1-4
Nehemiah 5-13
Malachi

Made in the USA
Middletown, DE
07 October 2018